PIECES OF IMAGINATION

PIECES OF IMAGINATION

RAYMOND CAMPBELL

MILL CITY PRESS
MINNEAPOLIS, MN

Mill City Press, Inc.
322 First Avenue N, 5th floor
Minneapolis, MN 55401
612.455.2293
www.millcitypublishing.com

ISBN-13: 978-1-63413-694-5
LCCN: 2015913869

Cover Design by James Arneson
Typeset by Emily Keenan

Printed in the United States of America

Contents

The Light of Tears

The tear and feeling walk hand in hand
As lovers
Pitying those who forgot how to cry,
Those who leave their tears
Strewn inside their memories
Like toys on the floor of a child's room.

A new tear wants to be embraced
And cradled softly close to the eye
That first nudged it into view
And revealed the presence of emotion.

Tears escort pieces of feeling
One by one
And lead them from the heart
To become performers on a stage of cheeks
Where others will know to look,
Then react with empathy or indifference.

Tears are small lights sliding toward love
While time floats next to them, smiling,
Waiting for tear and feeling to join as one.

The Funeral

Jim was the last adult male in the family.
I was the only child.
Now the women, except my mother,
were standing together on the grass.
Men in uniforms shot rifles in the air.
A flag folded into a triangle
was carefully placed in the hands
of my grandaunt Nell, his sister.

Later at home I went to her empty bedroom.
I picked up the flag cautiously.
Since my father died last year, a few weeks after my third birthday,
Jim was my new father,
now a flag and memories.
I knew he was in a war and his lungs were bad.

I unfolded the flag so no part was hidden.
It was very large; I looked at it for a while,
not understanding its meaning,
but knew it was important.
I touched it and admired it, rearranged it on the bed.
I started to refold it the way it should be.

It would not fold right.
I tried to remember
but couldn't see how the folds went.
I fumbled and cried but couldn't make the triangle.
My aunt Nell walked in, looked at me and the flag.
She wasn't one to say much about things but I dreaded what she might say
about this. Her face didn't change. She seemed to know what happened.
It's okay, she said.

Snow in the Woods

The frigid stillness begs to be touched by finger or tongue,
to be kissed like snowflakes do
while they float through brittle air
where they like to tease your eyes with cold dots
when you look up at them.

Fir trees pull their wooden sinews taut
to keep their limbs stretched,
cradling flakes above the ground
where they can better mute the sounds
to sculpt a lullaby without words that lures a child to sleep.

It seems perfect to be alone so no one makes a noise
to disturb the profound presence of silence
which the firs and snow leave intact when they capture the sound
and hide it somewhere or simply iron it flat with the weight of cold air.

Feather Song

The small bird's throat quivered
as it swiftly grabbed pieces of air
and yanked them back and forth
until I heard them tremble as waves of sound.
The notes were more potent than Diana's arrows
as they darted in all directions simultaneously
but could not be seen.
They easily found me without warning
and used my eardrums as trampolines for the bird's air.

Listening to the bird needed no effort or invitation.
Its sound required no key or combination.
The bird trilled a language
used by creatures of the air.

Scientists probe these sounds
for conclusions they pack in hard drives and iClouds
and analyze the sonic mechanics.
The bird embraces the air with faith
and is satisfied with its own vocabulary.

The throat stilled.
The bird flew into quiet, its natural camouflage,
where it rests, nearly invisible,
until it again sings its imposing pleasure.

A Piece of Eternity

Eternity does not happen quickly.
It cannot even be recognized
if it is divided into chapters
that seem individually wrapped and finite
but are quietly linked to worlds without end.

Groans protest the discomfort of such thoughts.
A foreboding voice says it's a glimpse
through a lens of imagination
at a world that will end sometime
on the day of God's disappointment
at hearing the desperate plea of prayers
begging Him to negate death,
a blemished way to end our familiar present.
Those souls who use prayer to complain
are not open to a new gift of existence
even though it is equipped with senses suited to a new odyssey
where we will inhale a world
and be free to choose balance or excess.
That freedom will be our infrastructure,
ensure that we will be creatures worthy of respect
or at least regarded as being of interest,
regardless of how our realities are structured.

We see our world as our senses interpret.
We host a gift whose history we don't recall,
like a goose on its maiden migration.
Can destiny have another gift waiting, similar yet different,
that will continue the sense of purpose we crave?
The words that feed meditation are not desperate for a new faith.
They are sounds in the cave where a new lens hibernates.

A Different Spot

Butterflies are beautiful but elude the human eye
if it tries to trace their paths.
I wonder what the world looks like
to the butterfly as it bounces and swerves
flipping perspective around like a lost pancake.
What would I see if I could duplicate its twisted course?

How do their eyes stay synchronized with bouncing wings?
It would be easier for us to observe and learn
if the wings would be more fixed and provided
a smooth and proper glide path
as nature does for other air creatures
and as humans design in their artificial machines.

But, if their wings became manageable for our observation
what would their eyes and brains do to maintain their sensibility?

They push air with outrageous wing motion.
If that no longer worked, they couldn't fly.
Earth and air would have to do the bouncing and twisting to keep
them airborne, a more than equally outrageous imitation
to substitute for the lost propulsion.
Our world would become an erratic propeller for butterflies.

I wish that Einstein, instead of watching a cart from a hill to conclude things
about light, had instead sat a little closer to flowers that lured butterflies
and started to contemplate qualities of light from the motion of butterflies.

We might have pilots, air traffic controllers, and navigators in constant argument.
Nightmare passes would have replaced airline tickets.

Maps would look like a crazy professor's painting of chaos.
Butterflies would assume enormous importance as the algorithm of travel.

I watch a butterfly that weaves a kaleidoscopic view
which might have been the gift
to lead Einstein to a different perspective on light
if he had rested at a different spot.

Promise the Rain

She is awakened by sounds
fiery with flashes
that backlight skyward beasts of burden
overloaded with sieves of water
she reads as rain.

She looks out at a formless gray blanket
waiting for it to shape to something she knows,
watching through drops
that twist jagged light into angles
to reveal reflections of her eyes
grabbing brightness in bursts.
She feels her eyes wriggling with translucence
as they struggle to embed the scene.

The once-molten sand she dreamt was crystallizing
on its way to glass
spews fermenting grapes in her throat
forcing her to exhale them as words
to tell the rain to hard quench the labeled bottle she holds,
as it can be held only once,
to make mirrored prison walls to point her light inward
where she and the storm will co-exist genie-like,
tightly corked against the vapor of escape.

She belongs to the storm now.
She can't be taken from it.
The storm pushes thunder inside her that
forces her hearing to escape boundaries, to sense aroma and flavor
as if she had prayed to taste the storm.

Loneliness and fulfillment meld to one
which she yearns to have brush close
as familiar wanting
before she remembers it as a dream.

Her nose again pressed against the pane
she watches the full brightness of lightning
moving wherever it wants,
unchanged by invention, with no wires to obey.

She must speak to it.
She hurries out into the storm
which drenches her in water and intermittent darkness.

She points her voice straight and strong into the storm.
I will be with you, closer than now.
I will embrace my true nature, as you do yours.
I will surge through reality and stand pressed to you.

We will dine on eternity together.

If you stay.

On the Water

The lapping against the hull that floats me
strokes sounds of contentment and reserves space
for the memory.

Above, a sail reaches toward white clouds
and attaches to the breeze that pushes it
gently toward a lullaby of motion.
The tiller rests in palm grip,
firm but relaxed in its command of direction
and reads the pull of the forces that work together
and oppose one another
as they interpret the wind.

Weightless splashes of water
raise a misty spray
that loves to find and caress your face.
A glance sternward pleasures at the swirl of wake
hypnotically kissing the hull good-bye.

Rounding the island tip finds wind change
and gradual rolling waves
that stir a thrill of challenge with ups and downs
birthing sounds so light and airy
they become interpreted as silence.

Snorkel and mask ring the mast base,
teasing hints of sharing a world
beneath the surface.

Whisper Carving

Wait for whispers that arrive at ear's edge
where you can carve new whisper faces before
they find passage to your mind.
Shape them sensitive, let your anticipation
form them as artful satisfaction.
Do it before your lover spoils your heart's welcome
and wastes it on rejection using words you do not like.

You can only catch the whisper at ear's edge.
That is where the artistry finds sanctuary to create
and the whispers learn they are not unchangeable,
where homely words are transformed to things of beauty
for which you waited, knowing how you would use them,
even though they are hard to visualize as you carve an abstraction.
You understand their clarity as they find a seat in your mind.

Finally you inhale the friendly reshaped words
and embrace them as if the sender intended their new tenderness.

Love's Presence

Love doesn't want to escape.
I capture it note by note,
word by word.
I breathe love and
drink songs that swirl within it.

Other hearts tune our music
after waiting to listen
for the moment it first sounds.
Sometimes it rings pure and undeniable,
then morphs into a solid.
I see it run along sun shadow's edge
which Earth captures as continuous nightfall
while it rotates to watch us glance at each other
swallowing the ride.

Love finds sadness all around it
painted in harsh hues,
and softens them with pastels
to be touched by tender light,
to soothe the ache, massaging it,
perversely ignoring time tugging
taut muscle until it excretes
a passion to be overworked,
mined of sensation.

Backwater Bridge

The bridge looks like a stationary bunch of steel
shaped to look pretty enough for a muddy river location
in a backcountry spot
that needs crossing as much as a Verrazano or a Golden Gate does.

Some of it yields to rust spots
as busy as termites on wood.
But sometime before it falls
painters will prolong it.

Pieces of it have fancy names like struts and such
but they all look like dumb steel that folks have to trust.

If you look way inside the surface of any of its parts
you might see it is a trap for forces
that want to push it down into the muddy water.
The trap begins with gravity that pulls in one direction.
The members do their job of dividing the tonnage into conquerable weights
that get spread out like fingers on a hand
poised in precise angles so the muscle doesn't fail.

A vehicle gets to the other side and wonders why it didn't break something, then is driven away out of sight. The bridge returns to a deserted portrait, feeling it was soothingly adjusted by a chiropractor. The fish and other wildlife are unimpressed.

All the traps are still in place, hidden by the dumb façade
of an old backwater bridge, muddy water sliding below quiet air,
washing along the pilings, which appear stoic and unknowing.

Blood Relatives

The corpses are the remains of
sons, fathers, brothers, uncles, friends,
all treasures of close relation and acquaintance
now on grassy hills bordered by trees
and undergrowth where they killed each other.
Where are the birds, the animals?
The men bleed or already bled
the stains that cover leaves and grass
which gurgled the screams that separated
into blue and gray.

The blades of grass feel the red fluid dripping from above
and oozing up from saturated dirt below
on which they lay blessed now in blindness
that they will not be forced to see
the soul of each man replayed,
the end of constant touches and nurturings
the mothers gave with love that breathed into
the food, the reading, the hugs and kisses,
the knowing of the strengths and grudging
acknowledgment of some weaknesses
which they tried to repair with encouragement.

All of that intricate love was not intended to sculpt a meager stone
that could merely point to the place of closure
where death gives permission to living mothers only to be visitors.

Can't Reach

Kathy wanders by on the school path
pretending she doesn't see me.
Her feet make the same tracks as any school day,
leading to where she finds strong belonging,
believes it is truth,
and listens to its choirs agree with her.

I find my reflection in pooled water
nestled close to woods
where I sing solo from memory.

The separate feelings are embedded in us
as we hunt different destinations
but know we could
share a steak, raise a family,
let the children choose
the world of school awards
or woods,
or both.

She will find a valedictorian in a city.

I will settle near a trout stream,
tie my own flies.

Chair

Empty seat beside me

waits for Nietzsche

while I whisper to a howling storm

that won't exist unless he's gone

Epitaph

This day I would not drive by as I have nearly every summer day
for the past decade. I stop to visit the nearly hidden cemetery in
Whittier, NC,
curious about the words on stones,
all that remains of many stories.
As I read them I started to think about what my epitaph should be.

Fantasy can be fun, so I imagined these words:
"Who was this interesting poet?
How did we miss him?
He made it easy, he missed us."

I was not actually planning a grave
but the idea bemused me enough
that I visited a stone carver
and showed him the words.
He looked at them, too quickly I thought,
and told me it was too long to chisel
into marble of reasonable size.
He said to come back in a few days.
A bit mysterious, but he seemed to imply a solution.

When I returned, the carver handed me four slips
of 3" x 5" paper, each one containing a short verse.
I scanned them and found one somewhat acceptable.
It read simply "I missed you."
Not a clear or inspiring message
but it did contain the essential words.
Alas, their true meaning would be hidden.
But they would fit.

I told him I liked that one,
folded it and put it in the breast pocket of my T-shirt.
I would keep it
in case I changed my mind about a grave.

First Bond

There are only two small rooms on the first floor.
She sits in the doorway that separates kitchen from living room,
Which now has her bed in it.
She can't go upstairs to sleep or use the bathroom.

Her daughter, the breadwinner, is at work.
She is nearly alone, except for her grandson whom she is told to guard
All day because age three is too young to roam outside alone.

The boy's father, her only son, died upstairs a few weeks ago.
The mother is still in the TB sanitarium so she can't help with her son.
Responsibility falls to the grandmother because she is the only one left.

The stool she sits on is wooden with four legs and a hard round seat.
Although her mind and body are struggling with age,
She knows she must keep her grandson in the house.

She holds a yardstick with quiet dignity.
She has never used it but it is a symbol of authority.
Despite her conscientious dedication, some escapes happen.
Her mobility is no match for a youngster.

There is no phone, no way to communicate with anyone.
She scans the small kitchen and sees no sign of her grandson.
She calls his name repeatedly.
No response.
At that moment, no one in the world knows what she is thinking or doing.
She is not sure herself.

The local Catholic school accepts her grandson at age four
After he is found bleeding badly by an older boy.

Now the family knows where he is,
But they have no insight to her world.
Now she spends her days alone.
No one to speak to or guard or watch play with his cat.

She thinks about her grandson.
She knows she loves him
And that he has seen her as no one else has in the past few months.
For a while he shared her end days,
The finishing of her life.

Graveyard

I cannot leave this place.
My feet are anchored in its soil
where ancestors wait for rescue
from anonymity.

Not even a scratched name or a piece of wood
has betrayed their last bed.

Some have stories that are repeated
on rare occasion,
some have only lost stories
that burrowed unseen into the ground
next to them.

Their spirits fared much better we believe,
though some are puzzled by the
deteriorations that continue in that different world.
Priests and those of mystical sensibility
will help them divine a destiny.

But I am chosen as the watchdog at the graveyard.
I actually have a title.
It is "Graveyard Dog."
I like to think my role was sketched
in the spirit of tongue in cheek,
although that would leave the puzzle of sorting out
what was serious.

My words are becoming more understandable to me.
Maybe I am dying too, or already dead,
lying beside those I am expected to guard.
I wonder if they have changed my title.

Denali Campfire

Sometimes a campfire is the only place for special communication
where strangers, family, friends, or acquaintances
display small or clever talents or insights,
each a tidbit with value in its own right
that condescends to pile up with other bits to
form a unique, interesting pile
that can amuse, invent perspective,
and help those firewatchers
sense that there is a stream of participation
that runs through all of them as they share each other
and the flame on coals
until physical calm and tiredness
peel them away from the warmth one by one
to sleep with a vague tranquility suggestive of accomplishment.

Apocalypse of Survival

This is the past he must escape and run to the future.
He wriggles through seagrass and clinging weed
trying to subdue his reaction to unreliable appearances
and tries to slither toward the spiritual
forces he has been told are here,
close to matters of the soul.

Friction is everywhere, armored with Earth's forces.
Seeing only superficiality pries open starved sensors
and squeezes them through pores as remnants of struggle.
He resents the thinness of truth, the need to kill to eat,
knowing even plants express urgency
to exist and not be devoured.

He struggles harder to be free
but finds himself expressed as part of
rising mountains and destructive melt.
He knows he is feeling the crush
of aggressive mountains that have pinned
his feet and press his body until
only his mouth and a partial eyelid
protrude from a small niche.
He tries to speak but there are no thoughts
to move the parts that create sound.

The gelatinous lid is pinched open a slit.
The sliver of light looks/feels familiar.
The brain stirs, senses that it might
have become part of this mountain too,
and missed its epiphany again,
still forced to hope for mere existence.

FEELING OUR EYES

Your eyes pointed at me,
Their blue soaring across the room
To softly dilate my eyes like a kitten reshaping a ball of yarn.
I let all your light pour in without resistance, willing to be captured.

Our eyes drew so close
We could not know if we sensed vision
Or our eyes were melting into one pool.

As space between us evaporated
Our lips touched
Surprised to find our eyes already in an embrace.

When our lingering lips withdrew
The parting was untraceable
Except for the forever blue you painted into my eyes
As indelible memory
Always able to be seen.

Her Time

I do not want to use words
that place her in a time that has already ended.
I want to see her in new things that we are both connected to
and still share the now I know she lost.

Time is the web that traps existence
in a shape that cannot be understood.
Where does it hide a life forever
with unchangeable certainty of no return?

Finding Humility

Martha wears uniform-like cloth,
looks like part of an unfamiliar sect
and works among the poor whose
needs give them and Martha strong magnetism
which others admire though not in their gut
where they could understand it.

Blake comes to this secluded spot for its peace,
massaged by the burble of water.
He thinks of Martha as he walks quietly, puzzled by her plainness.
He notices a few blades of grass move and sees a snake.
The blades lose their motion, wait for something to push them.
The library book that Blake read explained why the snake is good,
a needed part of our world.
Blades of grass begin to stir again and part slowly
as the snake moves, tongue flickering ahead.
Blake sits quietly, cannot pretend even to himself
that he does not have a primitive urge which ignites a prejudice.
He can taste the regurgitated memory of the book with repugnance.

Blake feels an empty twinge
that fills with Martha's image.
Everyone admires her but for false reasons, like those in the library book.
They don't see that she has rejected normal life,
the kind that is good enough for the rest of us.
As Blake thinks, the snake stops,
seems to look at him.
He thinks that Martha is more like the snake, not the angel people think of.

The snake flicks its tongue and starts to move away unafraid.
Blake sees it anew as just a creature being a snake

and wonders why Martha doesn't accept being an ordinary person,
enough of a gift for most of us.
As Martha moves into history, image on the rise,
the snake crawls into anonymity humbly accepting what it is.

This Cat

Reflexively I assess the black fur for clues of bristle.
This cat's eyes peer back.
The stuff inside is mirrored out
as unapologetic messages, intent unreadable.

Her eyes leave no doubt they see and feel
and are suspicious of what mine reveal.
She is thinking.
This assessment is allowed time to shape
only because our relationship
tolerates the reading of our moods.

Claws or purrs are hair-trigger options.
This cat has no taste for predictability.
It reserves the right to require respect,
an expectation it presages with absence of fear.

Her tail starts to move, not fast and twitching,
not too slow like a stealthy lure.
Tail language says a purr will follow.
We are friends today.

Summer Sunset in Whittier

Birds praised the dimming of sun heat
and frequenced their songs to thicker density
that fit day's end better than brightness.
Dusk is a ready welcome to the cool light sprinkled by fireflies
who want to express their destiny briefly
and not stay for the nightly choir.
The active part of their day is short,
even if you count the time they queue just below the dirt's surface
waiting for that brief space of time between birds and cicadas
in which they sparkle and breed.

The cicadas also waited but with a bit more patience,
yielding time for birds to sing their share
and mute the silence that slid opposite daylight.

For a while the birds seem to grow in number,
then begin to retire before they are saddled
with the burdens of being nocturnal.

Stones and Kites

I paste words on kites that will take them
where others can see they are not reflections of symbols in books
with pages of knowledge out of focus
and meaning tainted by mold before I taste its sweetness.
My kites fly only new thoughts at a comfortable pace.

I write faster when I want to see more
but the pen skips the surface
like a stone thrown by a boy who counts the skips
and winces at the image of stones sinking fast.
Not much contact with the surface
which is where appearance reveals itself
and the water's glisten becomes a ghost.

This is when I slow to let words and thoughts marry
after they find natural couplings
and ignore prearrangements they are told are needed.

Words can exist wild in our nature
as animals do in their habitat
where they are praised for being feral
and have not been lured to cages.

Shallow

I like to stay at the surface of things
where faces of wood or skin show attraction,
where I don't see the world of dirt underneath
filled with slimy feedings and maggots.

I am content to let vegetation suck
beneath the places I like
and push mucky nightmares
up into sunlight
where they will sophisticate into things
meant to be seen and touched.

Ruth says I miss a lot and am superficial
in my tasting of life,
a reticence I will regret.
Her words make blank my belief
that she, as a woman,
would be the one to expect things beautiful
and avoid immersion in the aesthetically sordid.
When my conversation occasionally ventured
to base levels that smeared even my own sensibilities
I thought I saw disgust in her eyes.
Now I see my impression as sexist oversimplification.

Do I only live at fussy or crude
and miss a boundary that separates the two
to segregate a balanced sanctuary
which I now see she expects me to inhabit?

I thought Ruth and I rode similar wavelengths
but our vows lasted only six months.

EMERGE

You never noticed I was different than I appeared,
someone else trying to emerge.
Neither of us knew me.
I wasn't completed yet,
and some parts won't ever be.
Their stems to nourishment atrophied
and fell to the ground like early dying leaves,
each beautiful color given permission by death.

The leaves never get to see their own beauty
or know if there would be any artful qualities that would display.
They could have looked at the others
and known that death precedes beauty for leaves.

I see something coming
that must bloom before death.
Who knows what life will express
when it takes shape.

It reaches through black frigid liquid
and grasps the self that sucks through
its own heart and knows it is the
strongest thing inside, puzzled by
its strength to exclude all other views.
Only self is the point from which all
interpretation of reality proceeds.
Each creature is its own epicenter.

Such is the force that blows headwinds at love.
I should have known
I would not emerge through that,
just as the leaves will never see their own colors.

At First Glance

She looks at her glass thinking
it never stays at the same level,
always being emptied or filled.
It is not important but the thought mesmerizes her,
even though her drink has no alcohol.

Others can see she looks untroubled without affectation.
She carries an innocence that
is partly masked by thin, long lashes
and a hint of a smile ready to laugh softly.

She knows men are glancing at her
and she pretends to ignore it.
She is glad to be attractive,
yet uncomfortable at the attention,
even though it is politely disguised.

I am attracted, part of those who glance,
and force myself to ask why I am here
where the superficial has already
pushed ahead of allowing a fair chance
to learn her values and deep preferences
which are so much more rewarding to discover.

After I order another drink
I turn back to see she is gone.

A Painted Moment

Daniela is wearing a light-blue dress with white lace at the sleeves
 and neck.
It doesn't look modern. It is more classical and seems to reverberate with the flowers she sits next to, all of them blurred as if their ink dripped through an Impressionist's brush.
She leans in with the flowers, not to pluck, but for their closeness
 and touch.
Her hair is silky, dark blonde, nearly shoulder length, which seems longer than most four-year-olds'. It is topped by a sunbonnet.
Flowers speak in color and textures. She feels their language.
She and they are related at the sensitive and innocent level of love,
a peaceful harmony of girl and
flowers, which know her large eyes are absorbing them.
Occasionally a tiny finger touches them. They seem to snuggle into
 the contact.

My sister sent me to fetch Dee from the backyard for lunch.
But my task is superseded by the chance to appreciate Daniela.
I hear my sister's voice ask if we are coming in.
Of course, I say, without moving.

A small snake moves at the edge of the flower bed, only a harmless
 ring neck.
Auntie April, a snake.
I stand and pick her up.
Yes, that's a harmless ring neck snake but it is a good idea not to let snakes
 get close.
In Florida some of the prettiest snakes are poisonous.
What's poisonous? Daniela stares up at me.
I'll tell you at lunch, Dee, I say,
as I hug her tight and carry her to the wooden steps.

A Storm Elsewhere

The hurricane will not get close
though it patters the windows' glass drums
and lets the panes set a mood.

All the preparations are done.
There is nothing left but to watch and listen.

In the distance the eye scans pain
which randomly forces itself into hiding lives.
It does not bring the ambience of soft sounds and candlelit dinner.
It brings approaching destruction complete with nature's weapons of fear.

While people here sleep well
and will awake with faded empathy,
people there have a sleepless night
fearing the census of loss to be counted
in the foreboding morning.

There won't be all the help that's needed,
nor will it be on time
but it will be what we must do.
Let's wake those who slept well,
then find those the storm ravished.

Dew Ewe

I love the dew, do you too?
I stand with you among the dew
and watch the ewe,
as their hooves strew new islands in the dew
as a ewe is wont to do.

We wait for the ewe to lick the drops
but the ewe chomps the whole clump of grass
including its dew too, due to the nature of the ewe.

The tiny spheres of light are becoming
fewer drops of dew as the sun herds them home
for a cup of dew tea
while there is still enough dew for the brew,
before the dew becomes two few.

They heard the herd command and leave and we do too,
and bid the dew adieu and wave to the ewe.
I wonder if the dew did the rhyming or was it ewe?

Imagination

Nothing there.
It's groaning for shape,
light streaming around it
not too close or sound will not follow.
It uses light and leaves a trail of gray.
The gray things covet some of the light for color.
Things do not live without color.

Texture can't resuscitate it from its feeble fingerhold.
The whole thing needs a new beginning,
A ledge for texture to teeter on,
perception to resolve its faults,
taste that could make a difference.

All these things are churning in the mire
where something seems to be gaining air
in a first breath, poking a tentacled eye
out of a swamp of adversity,
disheveled and misshapen,
grotesquely taking its first step,
hopeful of repenting into a new soul
and asserting its own space in reality.

Still a carrier of ugliness
it does not want to be pronounced dead by a censor.
It knows it can grow to be loved as imagination.

Last Poem

The last stroke of pen will say things
I didn't do with life.
I'll look at only the actual path,
not things that were unseen
but things I did see and knew
I had gifts to be more.

It is not time yet.
I have too many voids to fill before the blanks become permanent
and it ceases to matter.
The spaces let flow
things that were mired in inactivity,
blind to the pillars that reached for a roof to complete my structure.

I recall others who tasted life as their own feast,
and those like me who glanced off the world as a voyeur,
who wanted to be knit into that fabric
but had perspectives more distant,
not similar or group-welded. Held in place by the membrane of a bubble
always ready to burst.

As my inward vision poked free
and let me feel the atrophy of not riding the world,
I saw it is too late to change the clouds of inertia
visible horizon to horizon to permit no blue.
But I have learned the meaning of fate
and know that I will look away from failure,
stay ready to fill the spaces that still arrive daily
and fill them with substance that transcends
the now lifeless clutter that could have been a treasury
of recollections of the past.

Movie Watcher

The handsome guy,
The beautiful woman
Find each other on the screen again and talk and show love.
They were selected for the screen.
I've already paid for this performance
But I keep coming back.

They melt into the moment and profess love.
I suspend disbelief and allow myself no reality questions.
They speak the same words but in a way I can never imitate.
I envy their beauty, their voices, the way they project truth.

Then I flash back to reality. This always happens in the same scene.
I hope some day to get beyond that point.
My feelings linger to light up memory.
I swear I hear a window slam shut,
The noise closes off the screen, the outside, and there ends
The young love the way I like to see it.
I am left in the theatre alone,
Knowing that I will pay again for the same performance.

Mist

Drops of water shrink part way until fatigued
and rest as tiny tired thirsty spheres,
not yet dry.

They hold specks of water tightly,
still able to blur images,
still able to stay aloft as damp kites.

They sneak small drinks
to plants, insects, or mammals
with gifted tongues.

The drops sip the sky at night
and sleep until dawn
when they let the sun
rub their ink away
until they disappear into the heat of day.

Old Man Thinking

The old man sat on the bank
of the shallow tributary.
He struggled with his shabby straw hat
to block the bright reflection.

He remembered when he plucked the faith out of mysticism
like plucking and discarding feathers of a fresh kill.
He wanted certainty that surely God could furnish
without room for doubt
unless there is a reason to cloud transparency.

He never found certainty nor the lost faith
and chose to straddle the explanations of existence,
like crossing a stream
always shifting weight to the next stone,
knowing he would never reach the other bank.

Word Lens

My view is different through your words
as if you changed my vision as I read them.
I give them breath, then lend my pen to them
but they are aware of your perception.

I like to learn but not know if they are your thoughts
or points on your compass that guide mine
or start to stir them toward creation.
So things I read have different shapes and hues,
aware they started on a canvas you have loaned.

I look out at trees and the sky shaped with clouds
and wonder what I would see if you described them first,
and I guess at whether we could converse in poetry,
or if the words have intangible hands
that I could take in mine and dance in silence.

Screech a Secret

Relaxed in the calm of the blue sky day
my eyes are awakened by the outline of a bird of prey
perched atop a dead tree. She starts a piercing call
while her talon clenches a fresh fish.

An osprey, proud of its catch, repeats its call.
Maybe she wants to share, but more likely brags her triumph.
It's hard to tell why she enjoys her noise.
I won't have time to find out the slant of her pleasure.
Even if I knew what to look for
she's going to keep her loud secret.

Soldiers Sacrificed

We cannot march in today's parade
nor participate in the flow of time.
That is owned by you now.
We provided the loss of our lives.
It is up to you to prove the gain
and live the reward of freedom.
We did our job and mailed you the paycheck.
Spend it with the hearts we trusted you would have.

Our flag is not lifeless dyed cloth.
It was the only symbol we could grasp
as we died hoping it would mean as much to you.
If you would mourn our loss of life,
if you would respect the value of our death,
look at it as we did when we handed you
the mantle of victory and the time to carry it
where we can no longer go.

South Windsor Storm

"No piecework today, 60 cents/hour" straw bosses shouted.
Shreds of netting that had been shade dangled from poles and wires
that were supposed to hold them up to face the sun.
Now vacant spaces let sunlight spill
on many stems collapsed by hail the night before.
Tattered muddied tobacco leaves needed to be discarded
along with the chance to earn six cents/bend.
A few good pickers could occasionally do two hundred bends/day.
Now $4.80/day was max.
A few of us grumbled just as the big boss was walking up behind,
his body tense, voice loud.

He made it sound like I was an ally of the storm
and showed no loyalty.
"What does your father do?"
The knot in my stomach was instant.
The storm didn't stop last night, it echoed this morning.
"He's dead, sir." I felt my face tremble.
He turned and left.
I felt sick. I was glad he didn't fire me.
I still remember the lesson he taught me in those seconds.

I looked around at the destruction.
It seemed an impossible task but I copied what others were doing.
I reached for the pride I knew as one of the few two hundred benders,
but couldn't digest that the leaves I waited 'til age fourteen to pick
were gone.
Green leaves I learned to touch, count, and detach at each of my
heartbeats,
knees bound in burlap, pushing toward the next.

The Pasture

A strand of rusty barbed wire dangles from the post,
a relic rotting from the top, still attached to weathered wood underneath,
grayed with character, grain lines
like the face of an old man.

The cow chews casually, large eyes calmly interested
to gaze at me over the wizened fence.
Her eyes are steady and peaceful.
She seems intent on spending time leisurely looking.

A lone tree shades her.
She was focused on chewing hay when I arrived.
Now she is doing her version of multitasking.
Chewing doesn't need much attention.
Her perusal of my presence is difficult to assess in terms of energy used.
All in all it seems there is not much shift of effort going on
between the two activities.

She seems capable of entertaining herself
without the need to hunt or be wary of predators,
and appears unconditioned to quick survival responses,
except for the occasional tail thrust at little things
that taunt her serenity.

Time Vanishes

Value is how much something is desired,
often stated in currency.
But sometimes the measure is portions of heart
which have felt how far appreciation reaches through time
to find fullness in remembrance of a first glance
or the last flood of nostalgia.

A swell of feelings overpowers
the purse's attempt to contain genuine value.
The purse is forced to relegate itself to lesser treasure,
the replaceables, the fungibles
that can accumulate but do not digest into the soul as love does,
its presence often accented by flowers and a moving stream
which frame a display of deep experience.
The stream's water is firm and uncompressible.
It floats anything less dense, without questioning its value,
and carries it into a dimension ruled by time
with a promise it will float forever.

Time has the highest value of all things
and value cannot exist without it
even though time does no work nor floats any cargo.
Yet time is more mysterious than other forces
and slowly unwraps itself in a thin sheet that
has no buoyancy and becomes the past instantaneously
as if it can tolerate only a brief dose of reality.
It leaves a wisp of experience in its wake
which we try to grasp in cupped fingers
but can sip only what is the past.

Shattered

The miniature cathedral, a porous lace of ceramic,
sheltered the garlic cloves.
The purest abrasive white fused around impossible amounts of air,
standing peacefully on the granite counter
content to display the few spicy cloves,
until the inadvertent nudge sent it plummeting
to hard, dense porcelain.

Its pieces scattered,
broken with no memory.
But it radiated an importance lying there.
A transient blink from the past,
a recent ancient ruin.
Something about it still exists
and captures interest.

I contemplated it for a while,
wishing it hadn't happened.
Some of its clay and air continued to wrap around
a hint of time and art
in a way I had not fully appreciated.
It looked sad, like a lover I had taken too much for granted
even though she held a pleasure I could feel.

Veneer split open,
it exposes more than I saw before.
Why did it have to break
to make me finish my thoughts about it?

Round Trip

I enter my birth river
with other salmon
against the current flow
that pushes lives and deaths.

I know this is a path I never travelled in this direction before.
It is my path, my direction now.

Eyes framed by brown fur
snorkel in my water and look at me.
I swim away fast.
There is a waterfall ahead,
a signpost of where I began this journey,
meant for me to point up into and jump,
which I repeat many times and at last near its crest
and feel the rush when I clear it
but not the jaws of the bear.

I barely feel my skin rip off,
am unaware of the digestion of my flesh.

Unknown to me, a jumper who was nearby finds her birth spot,
exactly where she once lay as a sperm-coated egg.
Successful as a navigator with invisible chart and compass
she rotates her tiny piece of the cycle
which fills a wild world
and obeys the edicts of an architect she might never know exists.

Surf Time

Serious discussion, spoken alone,
looks for answers, clues, purpose.
Sees a range from Mother Teresa to Hitler.
Probe deeply beneath skin
tunnel through flesh
push away obstructive nerves
infected with pain
to reach bone and find no epiphany
no sense of elation that sees reality heal.

It's not here, that stuff of vision.
It is in the swells at beaches.
It lifts, pushes,
loses the frigid shock of submersion
and drags you to some primordial space
where links to the past lap at you
and spill over your head
until you breathe salty water
that hints at history with relics
of afterbirth and liquids of predecessors,
escapees from the darkening silt of swirling clay
who elevate to crystal transparency above the murk
where exposed prey and unveiled art
bubble to motion of foam and power
and burst open a clearer path of insight to the world of water
engorged with feeling and celebration
perfect for the mood of a surfboard.

The Inside of Change

Change magnifies interest in itself,
pushing self-image to scale new plateaus
where a dimension of alluring visions
send new signals that others sense
and try to interpret.
This change moves in a series
of bursts and erratic thrusts
which hurl perspectives that evolve in meaning
and know they will become new
and never stand still nor let their movement
fall beneath the pace of destiny.

Hummingbird in Whittier

This hummingbird thinks I guard the feeder,
like he does, driving away others trying to feed.
He sits on only a few select perches
impossibly thin, too spindly to support a songbird.
He darts quickly sipping nectar through a tongue
as long as his beak while wings beat so fast
they fan my wonder if energy might be used
faster than a few sips can restore it.

A staccato baritone, like a chirp rasped with rhythm,
makes known a woodpecker's nearness, which is ignored as harmless.
Only bees and ants find the feeder/nectar pairing
to be a cafeteria worth a crowd.

Perches near the food source
seem to content the hummingbird
except when another hummer intrudes
to give chase or needs to be chased itself.

Dusk glums the sky and briefly hummers and fireflies
are visible at the same time.
Then, gradually, the fireflies are alone.
The scenery switches to sound
as cicadas seem to chorus everywhere.
When light's edge starts to disappear
the tiny birds sip greedily before their exit.
They leave the fireflies to be the lone display
for their short day of activity
which cicadas end by switching the night to audio.
Cicadas pump their chorus to full volume
and will hand the stage back to the hummers
when they return to feed at the hint of dawn.

Me

There was pain

birthing from another species

a reflection

when it spoke

it was my name

Oceans and Friends

I am surrounded in a sea of constant new sensitivities
which pound enticingly at the shores
and beg me to appreciate all that I see and hear.
Barely one inspiration is attended to
and others push at me and rush by me in waves
that jostle my balance.
Too many waves to capture
so I force myself to be content
to make friends of a few,
always tempted to look back
to wonder at those I couldn't fit
in my time capacity
and watched them pass out of sight
with a haunting promise
that they should have been included
with the friends I found the space to keep.
I know creativity will have to slow
to expand the time I have
to harbor any naïve hope to keep them all.

NO LINK FOR LOVE

In the airport at Anchorage her smile was easy and natural
Glowing beneath soft red hair which framed her openly displayed personality
That spoke it had nothing to hide.
Standing next to her was an accident of good fortune
And we began speaking as strangers sometimes do.

Moments later we found ourselves seated in the same row
But spaced so she was at one window seat and I at the other.
When our unexpecting glances met
She seemed no longer a stranger,
But an old friend I had begun to rediscover.

After landing in Minneapolis I found her nearby,
Learned we both had layovers,
And asked if she would like a coffee.
Somehow my conversation led to sharing
That my wife had passed two years ago
And she shared that she had lost her spouse ten years before.
I was startled that our conversation had leapt to something
Less casual than was customary.

As we finished our coffee, she asked how long my layover was.
I had assumed that there was at least a two-hour differential
Between Florida and Minneapolis, as was the case in Wisconsin.
But no, as I looked at the local clock I became confused.
I realized departure was in only twenty minutes
At a faraway gate.

At the same instant a spasm of guilt ripped me
With the shame of acting normal, as though I didn't have terminal cancer,
As though I had life I could share.

Although we introduced each other
Before I hurried off to my flight,
I don't think I ever heard her name.
It was good we didn't have more time to share.
I suddenly realized my time is no longer normal.
It is truncated without a future attached.
Like newborn life, the start of romance must have a link to time.

Opera

I did not like opera
until I stood close and saw
the music love in your eyes
as you listened from the hospital bed.

The soloist sent her voice through both of us.
It trilled high and soft.
I did not understand the words
but was moved to taste a tear
and feel the feeling.

You were supposed to attend the performance.
I promised to go with you,
but dreaded the commitment.
I am glad I brought the disc
that yields her song.
I know now how you enjoy it.

As I continue to smile at your face
I see your eyes become vacant
and know it was your last listen.

Pretense

The actor, unlimited by genuine feelings,
wanders a course around reality
contrived to suit his needs and wishes.

And why not. With such a captivating veneer
why strain to bind his image to moral accuracy when his current method
already soothes the shallow values he embraces.

His identity is but a pseudonym for his soul
which is able to paste laughter over a face of sadness
that expects admiration and requires submission
to what does not exist
and gives him what he covets
without the demands imposed by honest sincerity.

Shoes with Laces

The shoelace goes in perplexing paths
to reach some preordained position.

As a kid I couldn't track it.
Now it's so automatic I still don't think I know its path.

But it doesn't matter; it ends up in the right position.
Well, maybe it does still matter.
I don't have to cheat now,
like when I made the knot and stuck both ends in it.

It looked like a real bow to me,
but my mother inspected it.
It wouldn't untie right
and I was in trouble.
I didn't know it was so important.

Having to tie a bow and failing is bad.

Sound Change

When you step out the door
Into the new cold
To head for school not far up the hill
You feel a difference in the sound
That is not there every day.

The light sleet patters on your slicker
And you hear a nearby train whistle
Spreading its loneliness in a haunting groan
Like a giant bagpipe on wheels,
Alternately tugging and pushing your mood
Leaving an aftertaste that will linger all day.

Embracing the sound is like framing a painting.
It changes nothing while changing everything,
Except for the sound you will hear tomorrow.

Sudden Departure

I looked at her from the edge of a precipice
whose space fell to being in love
and watched her face mime rejection.

My memory slipped back to younger years,
but her rebuff was no softer then.
I ventured a question still hopeful for our direction
though I could feel the answer in my gut.
I begged her to consider that everyone thought we were close to being one
and asked why she had stayed so long.

She said it was too late to leave until now.
I tried to see that logic through her hardness,
remembered her whispers of endless affection.
She turned and left with my heart.

I stared at the emptiness beside me
which would become my friend.

Shared Vision

You see people's depths and edges,
hear their love and anxieties.
I learn to run and hide as survival,
don't see relaxed texture or friend comfort.

Your insights find understanding
that branches into wisdom with no fear in its sap,
builds roots below to support a tree
with soft shade for others to shelter under.

I seek distance from others
and find pleasure in the workings of things
that mostly don't plot or scheme,
instead follow a paradigm, not selectively,
but as nature bound them with inflexible law.

If we each could exchange one eye to mix our pairs
our different worlds would merge with more in common
or the eyes would become too-close neighbors
that are wreathed in argument for the full length of their history.

Logic and Mysticism

Look into the right delivery room
and you see logic is the birth canal of ideas.
Like the baby, they were put there by a passion of procreation,
free of fealty to some brand of mysticism
which comes later to twist the shape of truth
like congenital disease does with the genes of babes.

Logic is bland, noncharismatic, practical.
Mysticism makes the ideas compelling and contagious,
stimulating and irresistible, like life.
Logic does useful work through invention.
Mysticism lights the workspace so the work result is seen.
Logic inbreeds with the fabric of reality.
Mysticism flees from the boundaries of science
and forms a new order of reason with no history to gauge it.

The mind is a constant worker shaping either logic or mysticism,
even spawning one or the other at sleep,
always exploring for discovery,
lifting logic or hoisting mysticism.

MEMORIES AND IMAGES ONLY

She deals with memories
forged by experience.
Remembered feelings are the progeny
of experience in a time relived.
She labels them memories but they are more.

Her realities are whittled down to shavings
accumulated in piles that grow
as she learns to respect them
for what they were in their contemporary time
as well as the now in which they are her memories.
The pleasure sucks from the same root
that allows her to savor it again and again
until she remembers that way no more
and resorts to an album with a fluffy life mascot
staring from a cover,
just a happy little rabbit on a hill wearing a smile,
every strand of fur captured as art,
painted inside her mind like a cave drawing
but less crude, less permanent, less seen,
more hidden by a coded entrance,
less a memory, more a book of fixed images.

Riding Sensitive

A freshly tearful memory,
a sad story worded by a recent book
reflects itself from every object in the room
and from things not here I yearn for
though only as a seldom ritual.

My loyalty to specific beauty is part time,
not vital to breath or heartbeats,
though it seems it should be
to conform to standards of intensity
I tell myself I live with.

Reflexive surges of sensitivity
temper any reluctance to feel love and empathy
until the flow of feeling needs rest
and steeps untasted flavors for a while
recouping for the next wave of artistic feeding.

Insight

all the dogs are boys
all the cats are girls
obviously

it was years before my
insight to biology
righted itself
a little

there seemed something right
and natural
about my old view

newer concepts
do explain
late night yowling
sound like fights

that speck of knowledge
meager payment
for the solid old reality

that speck marched in
like a foot soldier
leading an army
of complex data

that spoils everything
unless you need to know

I miss
the dog-boys
the cat-girls

Trap-Door Spider

I am *Pachylomerides audouini*.
I am a trap-door spider.

I live here in this dirt hole
with the flimsy flat roof.
I built it myself.
There was no school or teacher,
I just knew how.

I peek outside at times.
I see that there are other spiders.
Some of them weave splendid webs,
others hunt on the ground.
Their lives seem more romantic than mine.

I tried to make a web, but
it was more complicated
than a hole with a trap door.
Of course I don't ooze ideal web silk.
It comes out of me looking like quality silk
but does not become a web.

I do not hunt well either,
and I have a crippling fear of being
trampled by one of those big things with feet or hooves.
It is scary enough snapping open my door
and dragging in a creature
who might be deadlier than I am.
I have to kill the creatures quickly,
not having the best silk to tie them.

Like the web spider, I have to wait for food to arrive.
Not like a Domino's delivery person
who brings food whose taste is known
and there is a prearranged exchange,
after which the deliverer leaves.
My deliverer never leaves and the menu is always a surprise.
Very fresh, too.

When I get a little depressed, I think about decorating.
I get tired of spending every day
in a dirt hole with a plain hatch door.
But if I fancied up the place
it might discourage the critters who visit for dinner,
or should I say as dinner.

So I will sit in this dirt hole
with the flimsy hatch door
waiting for the vibrations of my next visitor
because I am *Pachylomerides audouini*;
I am a trap-door spider.

Tundra and Painting

I see a loose end of rope and try to pull but there is no resistance, no substance to it. There is a sled attached, dogs running toward the white horizon. I hold on waiting to be pulled somewhere. There is a face on the sled. If it speaks will I respond?
I don't think we would have anything in common except being out here on the tundra.

This is the wrong place to search for anyone who cares about the same things I do. I should be in a town or city with libraries and artists and groups that sing or discuss the weather, not live it.

Even a painting has more life even though it doesn't move or change. Some artist dabbed or bold-stroked pigment with color and texture, some strokes deliberate, some just pauses in inspiration. If nothing was put there it would be white space conspicuous by contrast. But the artist puts something there to disguise the absence of intended meaning, knowing most observers will not find anything to disclose its lack of purpose, will not see its incompatibility with other strokes. Most of the admirers will assign their own interpretation anyway, even to the intended strokes in proportion to the artist's reputation. Filling in the white spaces makes sense as I have learned, but it has its hazards, too, with promises of substance not there.

The painting hangs there seeming to look back at the appreciators who take the time to wait for their own reaction. But it is not looking. It is only a remnant of the artist's ability to tease, just hanging there passively letting others appraise its meaning. Some will want to buy it to possess a magic it does not share at any price. Others pass too quickly to be teased by any qualities it would appear to possess.

If there were a rope hanging from the painting would I try to seize it? Not likely. It would offer no resistance, as I have already learned. Whatever it might have of value, the rope will not be attached to it, will not pull meaning from it no matter how earnestly I might tug.

This is how I found the tundra where the certainty of finding nothing in common is nearly absolute.

Unguarded Smile

Uninhibited smiles are full orchestras
that burst with spontaneity
which joins innocence I did not know was there
until it flooded feeling into the spaces around it.

Gifted photographers love to capture things that
others don't see but then don't want to forget,
a glimpse that begs to be saved.
Others try to compress things into two dimensions
so they can corral them to be restricted and trained,
but which escape as full-dimensioned vision
that sheds its mask when teased by a smile.

Everyone in a crowd becomes more openly beautiful,
every instrument in the orchestra sings clearer
in the glow of a smile.

A string that binds the features too tight is untied
and lets their naked aspect tumble into unshielded visibility,
removed from barriers to let you see who they are.

It is an awakening to see a face
express that it is free.
You can touch the thread of their nature as it unfurls a common fabric
for those radiating a smile.
I love to watch a person who sees and hears kind humor
and lets themselves embrace it
with heart and open senses.

I wait for you to share your smile with me
if even for an indelible moment
so I can nestle in your heart and see it unguarded.

Until We Part

When I saw you, my eyes knew they could never let go.
Your voice drifted inside, only a thin membrane away
from the blood of my heart, which pulsed an exchange of love.

We went on picnics, sailed, water-skied, hiked in the Smokies
and made perfect love.
We saw things in each other's eyes
that would not let our awe find rest.
Your lips found the perfect way to taste
and you shared it unguardedly
until I no longer had more air to separate our breath.

Years later something happened.
You didn't last as long as the document stated.
You had died much before that.
You died before we said good-bye,
before we could speak one more time,
as I thought I knew we would.

Tippy's Lesson

He and his dog Tippy sit on the rocky edge of a field
filled with tall grass and goldenrod and the smell of early summer.
Everything is quiet except for the sound of crickets
and his occasional whispered words which Tippy cannot understand
but cocks her head side to side to show she is interested.

He wonders if it will work to be buffered from the real world
by endless filters
designed to prevent destructive mistakes and remove impurities.
Or do the deeds need their genesis to flow from a purer source,
their origin radiating from an energy
which nature imbued with moral compass and good nature?

He glances at Tippy and her priceless expression that she owned even as
a puppy.
Her body language and loving, innocent eyes
compel him to grin back at her and feel the purity of her nature
and realize that she is showing him the answer.

Time Won't Bend

It rips my heart that time won't bend
To scoop up happenings I want to capture and repair
With gentle attention to softness,
To undo pangs or longings
That ached in your heart
But could not sour your sweetness
So that you emerged more beautiful than a moonlit night
Hinting at dawn.

I cannot imagine that you could have bloomed more sensitively
Even if the hurt could have been extracted.
But I cringe that I was not there to try.

You who I have come to love more intuitively than anyone before.
You who sweetly wanted me to be a part of your life
Simply because you wanted me to be a part of your life,
But did not find me in it.

How could my pathway not have included you?
How could I have forged through life alone learning about pain
But did not see yours?
Why won't time bend
And let me find where the pathway should have led,
Where you were standing in the middle of it
And I could not walk around you?

The Waterfall

I sat on the riverbank.
The falls upstream were louder
than the water at this spot,
a different pitch too.

When it's in a glass it's quiet.
It takes a crowd of drops to make noise.

I tried to focus on an individual drop.
For a crazy second I wondered if one drop could be quiet
in a crowd. Sound seems to be a group activity for water
like it can only sing in a choir.

I was inspired.
If the rocks and pebbles and slope
beneath the moving drops
were arranged with skill and talent
they could produce music.
I could start with something simple like
"When you wish upon a star."
Scientifically it's perfectly feasible,
a simple water music box.

It would take something like a sluiceway
and patience. Pebbles and rocks are no problem.

I got tired of thinking about all that
so I got up to leave the spot.
Walking along the river I wondered if they were running from the hill
or to the sea and if they would become someone's drink.
All the while "when you wish upon a star" kept recycling
in my head.

I headed home like I was on autopilot
and lay down on my bed
hoping that I would dream
that I was a fellow drop.

What Man Is an Island

A few men are islands
conditioned through rejection,
forced to savor isolation
and enjoy the flavor.
It is difficult to feint motion toward concern
to appear akin to others.
It can be done, but the wake of its deceit
makes truth look like a hurricane has blown it down flat
like a field of sugarcane that was in its way and now lays prone
as a swath of collateral damage.

Caring hunters sense this
and refuse to accept the heartlessness
of a kill without the need to eat.
They retreat to their food-source morality
that soothes discomfort that was piqued
by the knowledge that others reject civility
and snuff out lives that were other creatures' friends or parents
and get off on the death in a rush of triumph
without regret and without nourishment.

But sensitivity survives in this artless jungle of compulsions
where it is written that alluring islands are its places of escape,
a natural habitat where the sensitive go to breathe alone
and nurse a different version of life
in which a poet can snooze peacefully
in the isolation from what appalls him.

But not much later he awakens and rejoins the society
rather than devolve into primitivism
and resumes living blended in with those
he wanted to reject
and becomes indistinguishable from them
after he rediscovers his own nature.

Next to Heaven

Nora feels the pain
of wet cold lapse to numbness
as she and her husband's lifejackets
keep them bobbing in the frigid North Atlantic.
As a woman passenger in first class
she was eligible for a seat on a lifeboat.
As a wife of over forty years
of time-tested love
she is eligible for a passage into death
with her loved one.

She and Robert exchange loving eye contact
and feel the wealth of life
which they distilled into a rare purity
they dared not hope for when first married.
Nora was too cold to speak
and wondered if Robert was thinking
of the same words as she,
"'Til death do we part,"
as her thoughts became frozen.

CPSIA information can be obtained at www.ICGtesting.com
Printed in the USA
LVOW07s1134101115

461513LV00004B/2/P